Poetry

Arthur Thomas Quiller-Couch

Contents

POETRY

BY

Arthur Thomas Quiller-Couch

POETRY
By
Arthur Quiller-Couch

"Trust in good verses then:
  They only shall aspire,
When pyramids, as men
  Are lost i'the funeral fire."

As the tale is told by Plato, in the tenth book of his **Republic**, one
Er the son of Arminius, a Pamphylian, was slain in battle; and ten days
afterwards, when they collected the bodies for burial, his body alone
showed no taint of corruption. His relatives, however, bore it off to
the funeral pile; and on the twelfth day, lying there, he returned to
life and told them what he had seen in the other world. Many wonders he
related concerning the dead, for example, with their rewards and
punishments: but most wonderful of all was the great Spindle of
Necessity which he saw reaching up into heaven with the planets
revolving around it in whorls of graduated width and speed, yet all
concentric and so timed that all complete the full circle punctually
together.--"The Spindle turns on the knees of Necessity: and on the rim
of each whorl sits perched a Siren, who goes round with it, hymning a
single note; the eight notes together forming one harmony."

* * * * *

The fable is a pretty one: but Er the Pamphylian comes back to report no more than the one thing Man already grasps for a certainty amid his welter of guesswork about the Universe--that its stability rests on ordered motion--that the "firmament" stands firm on a balance of active and tremendous forces somehow harmoniously composed. Theology asks "By whom?": Philosophy inclines rather to guess "How?" Natural Science, allowing that these questions are probably unanswerable, contents itself with mapping and measuring what it can of the various forces. But all agree about the harmony: and when a Newton discovers a single rule of it for us, he but makes our assurance surer.

For uncounted centuries before ever hearing of "Gravitation" men knew of the sun that he rose and set at hours which, though mysteriously appointed, could be accurately predicted; of the moon that she regularly waxed and waned, drawing the waters of the earth in a flow and ebb, the gauge of which and the time-table could be advertised beforehand in the almanack; of the stars, that they swung as by clockwork around the pole. Says the son of Sirach concerning them--

> *At the word of the Holy one they will stand in due order,*
> *And they will not faint in their watches.*

So evident is this celestial harmony that men, seeking to account for it by what was most harmonious in themselves or in their experience, supposed an actual Music of the Spheres inaudible to mortals; Plato (who learned of Pythagoras) inventing his Octave of Sirens, spinning in the whorls of the great planets and intoning as they spin; Chaucer (who learned of Dante and makes the spheres nine) in his ***Parliament of Foules*** telling, out of Cicero's ***Somnium Scipionis***, how the great

Scipio Africanus visited his descendant in a dream and--

Shewed he him the litel erthe, that heer is,
In regard of the hevenes quantite:
And after shewed he him the nyne speres,
And after that the melodye herde he
That cometh of thilke speres thryes-three
That welle is of musicke and melodye
In this world heer, and cause of armonye.

While Shakespeare in the last Act of **The Merchant of Venice** makes all the stars vocal, and not the planets only:

There's not the smallest orb which thou beholdest
But in his motion like an angel sings,
Still quiring to the young-eyed cherubims...

And Milton in **Arcades** goes straight back to Plato (save that his spheres are nine, as with Chaucer):

then listen I
To the celestial Sirens' harmony
That sit upon the nine enfolded spheres
And sing to those that hold the vital shears
And turn the adamantine spindle round
Of which the fate of gods and men is wound.
Such sweet compulsion doth in music lie
To lull the daughters of Necessity,
And keep unsteady Nature to her law,
And the low world in measured motion draw
After the heavenly tune.

From the greater poets let us turn to a lesser one, whom we shall have occasion to quote again by and by: to the ***Orchestra*** of Sir John Davies (1596), who sees this whole Universe treading the harmonious measures of a dance; and let us select one stanza, of the tides:

> *For lo, the sea that fleets about the land,*
> *And like a girdle clips her solid waist,*
> *Music and Measure both doth understand;*
> *For his great Crystal Eye is always cast*
> *Up to the Moon, and on her fixed fast;*
> *And as she daunceth in her pallid sphere,*
> *So daunceth he about the centre here.*

This may be fantastic. As the late Professor Skeat informed the world solemnly in a footnote, "Modern astronomy has exploded the singular notion of revolving hollow concentric spheres...." (The Professor wrote "singular" when he meant "curious."--The notion was never "singular.") "These 'spheres,'" he adds, "have disappeared, and their music with them, except in poetry." Nevertheless the fable presents a truth, and one of the two most important truths in the world. This Universe is not a Chaos. (If it were, by the way, we should be unable to reason about it at all.) It stands and is continually renewed upon an ascertained harmony: and what Plato called "Necessity" is the duty in all things of obedience to that harmony, the Duty of which Wordsworth sings in his noble Ode,

> *Thou dost preserve the stars from wrong,*
> *And his most ancient heavens, through thee, are fresh and strong.*

Now the other and only equally important truth in the world is that this macrocosm of the Universe, with its harmony, cannot be apprehended at all except as it is focussed upon the eye and intellect of Man, the microcosm. All "transcendental" philosophy,--all discussions of the "Absolute," of mind and matter, of "subjective" and "objective" knowledge, of "ideas" and "phenomena," "flux" and "permanence"--all "systems" and "schools," down from the earliest to be found in "Ritter and Preller," through Plato, Aristotle, Zeno, Epicurus, on to Aquinas, to Abelard, to the great scholastic disputants between Realism and Nominalism; again on to Bacon, Spinoza, Locke, Comte, Hegel, and yet again on to James and Bergson--all inevitably work out to this, that the Universal Harmony is meaningless and nothing to Man save in so far as he apprehends it, and that he can only apprehend it by reference to some corresponding harmony within himself. Lacking him, the harmony (so far as he knows) would utterly lack the compliment of an audience: by his own faulty instrument he must seek to interpret it, if it is to be interpreted at all: and so, like the man at the piano, he goes on "doing his best."

*   *   *   *   *

"God created Man in His image," says the Scripture: "and," adds Heine, "Man made haste to return the compliment." It sounds wicked, but is one of the truest things ever said. After all, and without vanity, it is the best compliment Man can pay, poor fellow!--and he goes on striving to pay it, though often enough rebuked for his zeal. "Canst *thou*," demands the divine Interlocutor in the ***Book of Job***--

"Canst thou bind the sweet influences of Pleiades, or loose the bands of Orion? Canst thou bring forth Mazaroth in his season? Or canst thou guide Arcturus with his sons?"

To this, fallen and arraigned man, using his best jargon, responds that "the answer is in the negative. I never pretended to *do* these things, only to guess, in my small way, how they are done."

Nor is there any real irreverence in answering thus: for of course it is not the Almighty who puts the questions, but someone audaciously personating Him. And some of us find this pretension irritating; as Douglas Jerrold meeting a pompous stranger on the pavement was moved to accost him with, "I beg your pardon, Sir, but would you mind informing me--Are you anybody in particular?"

Again, in the sixth chapter of the Second Book of Esdras, someone usurping the voice of the Almighty and using (be it said to his credit) excellent prose, declares:

"In the beginning, when the earth was made, before the waters of the world stood, or ever the wind blew,

Before it thundered or lightened, or ever the foundations of paradise were laid,

Before the fair flowers were seen, or ever the moveable powers were established; before the innumerable multitude of angels were gathered together,

Or ever the heights of the air were lifted up, before the measures of the firmament were named, or ever the chimneys of Zion were hot.

Then *did I consider these things, and they all were made through Me alone, and through none other: by Me also they shall be ended, and by none other."*

It is all very beautiful: but (for aught that appears) no one was denying it. It has been shrewdly objected against the arguments of the

"affable Archangel" in the later books of *Paradise Lost* that argument
by its nature admits of being answered: and the fatal fallacy of putting
human speech into a divine mouth, as in the above passage, is that it
invites retort.

A sensible man does not aspire to bind the sweet influences of Pleiades:
but he may, and does, aspire to understand something of the universal
harmony in which he and they bear a part, if only that he may render it
a more perfect obedience. "Let me know," he craves, "that I may accept
my fate intelligently, even though it prove that under the iron rule of
Necessity I have no more freedom of will than the dead,

> *Roll'd round in earth's diurnal course*
> *With rocks, and stones, and trees.*"

The claim (as Man must think) is a just one--for why was he given
intelligence if not to use it? And even though disallowed as
presumptuous, it is an instinctive one. Man is, after all, a part of the
Universe, and just as surely as the Pleiades or Arcturus: and moreover
he *feels* in himself a harmony correspondent with the greater harmony
of his quest. His heart beats to a rhythm: his blood pulses through
steady circuits; like the plants by which he is fed, he comes to birth,
grows, begets his kind, dies, and returns to earth; like the tides, his
days of gestation obey the moon and can be reckoned by her; in the sweat
of his body he tills the ground, and by the seasons, summer and winter,
seedtime and harvest, his life while it lasts is regulated. But above
all he is the microcosm, the tiny percipient centre upon which the
immense cosmic circle focusses itself as the sun upon a
burning-glass--and he is not shrivelled up by the miracle! Other
creatures (he notes) share his sensations; but, so far as he can
discover, not his intelligence--or, if at all, in no degree worth
measuring. So far as he can detect, he is not only an actor in the grand
cosmic pageant, but the sole intelligent spectator. As a poor Welsh

parson, Thomas Traherne, wrote of the small town of his childhood:--

The streets were mine, the temple was mine, the people were mine, their clothes and gold and silver were mine, as much as their sparkling eyes, their skins and ruddy faces. The skies were mine, and so were the sun and moon and stars; and all the world was mine, and I the only spectator and enjoyer of it....

> *But little did the infant dream*
> *That all the treasures of the world were by;*
> *And that himself was so the cream*
> *And crown of all which round about did lie.*
> *Yet thus it was: the Gem,*
> *The Diadem,*
> *The ring enclosing all*
> *That stood upon this earthly ball,*
> *The heavenly Eye,*
> *Much wider than the sky*
> *Wherein they all included were,*
> *The glorious soul that was the King,*
> *Made to possess them, did appear*
> *A small and little thing!*

We may safely go some way even beyond this, and lay it down for unchallengeable truth that over and above Man's consciousness of being the eye of the Universe and receptacle, however imperfect, of its great harmony, he has a native impulse to merge himself in that harmony and be one with it: a spirit in his heart (as the Scripture puts it) "of adoption, whereby we cry, **Abba, Father**"--And because ye are sons, God hath sent forth the Spirit of His Son into your hearts, crying, Abba, Father. In his daily life he is for ever seeking after harmony in avoidance of chaos, cultivating personal habits after the clock; in his civic life forming governments, attempting hierarchies, laws, constitutions, by which (as he hopes) a system of society will work in tune, almost automatically. When he fights he has learnt that his fighting men shall march in rhythm and deploy rhythmically, and they do so to regimental music. If he haul rope or weigh anchor, setting out to sea, or haul up his ship on a beach, he has proved by experiment that these operations are performed more than twice as easily when done to a tune. But these are dull, less than half-conscious, imitations of the great harmony for which, when he starts out to understand and interpret it consciously, he must use the most godlike of all his gifts. Now the most godlike of all human gifts--the singular gift separating Man from the brutes--is speech. If he can harmonise speech he has taught his first and peculiar faculty to obey the great rhythm: "I will sing and give praise," says the Psalmist, "with the best member that I have." Thus by harmonising speech (in a fashion we will discuss by and by), he arrives at *Poetry*.

*   *   *   *   *

But an objection may be raised. "Is the tongue, rather than the brain, the best member that I have?" or (to put it in another way), "Surely a man's *thoughts* about the Universe have more value than his words about it?"

The answer is, that we cannot separate them: and Newman has put this so cogently that I must quote him, making no attempt to water down his argument with words of my own. "Thought and speech are inseparable from one another. Matter and expression are parts of one: style is a thinking out into language. This is literature; not *things*, but the verbal symbols of things; not on the other hand mere *words*, but thoughts expressed in language. Call to mind the meaning of the Greek word which expresses this special prerogative of Man over the feeble intelligence of the lower animals. It is called Logos. What does Logos mean? It stands both for **reason** and for **speech**, and it is difficult to say which means more properly. It means both at once: why? Because really they cannot be divided.... When we can separate light and illumination, life and motion, the convex and the concave of a curve, then will it be possible for thought to tread speech under foot and to hope to do without it--then will it be conceivable that the vigorous and fertile intellect should renounce its own double, its instrument of expression and the channel of its speculations and emotions." Words, in short, are the outward and visible signs of thought: that, and something more--since you may prove by experiment that the shortest and simplest train of thought cannot be followed unless at every step the mind silently casts it into the mould of words.

*   *   *   *   *

As an instrument for reconciling Man's inward harmony with the great outer harmony of the Universe, Poetry is notoriously imperfect. Men have tried others therefore--others that appeared at first sight more promising, such as Music and Mathematics--yet on the whole to their disappointment.

Take Mathematics. Numbers inhere in all harmony. By numbers harmony can
be expressed far more severely than by Poetry, and so successfully up to a point, that poets have borrowed the very word to dignify their poor efforts. They "lisp in numbers"--or so they say: and the curious may turn to the **Parmenides**, to Book vii. of **The Republic** and others of the **Dialogues** and note how Plato, hunting on the trail of many distinguished predecessors, pursues Mathematics up to the point where, as a means of interpreting to Man the Universal harmony, Mathematics, like Philosophy, inevitably breaks down. Mathematics, an abstract science, breaks down just because it is abstract and in no way personal:

because though it may calculate and time and even weigh parts of the greater Universe, it cannot, by defect of its nature, bring its discoveries back to bear on the other harmony of Man. It is impersonal and therefore nescient of his need. Though by such a science he gain the whole world, it shall not profit a man who misses from it his own soul.

Philosophy, too, fails us over this same crux of "personality"; not by ignoring it, but by clinging with obstinacy to the wrong end of the stick. The quarrel between Philosophy and Poetry is notorious and inveterate: and at ninety-nine points in the hundred Philosophy has the better of the dispute; as the Fox in the fable had ninety-nine ways of evading the hounds, against the Cat's solitary one. But the Cat could climb a tree.

So Philosophy has almost all the say in this matter, until Poetry interjects the fatal question, "I beg your pardon, Madam, but do you happen to be the Almighty, or are you playing Egeria to his Numa? You are constructing admirably comprehensive schemes and systems for *His* guidance, if your hints will but be taken. But if you address yourself to Man, you will find that his business is not at all to *comprehend* the Universe; for this, if he could achieve it, would make him equal with God. What he more humbly aspires to, is to *apprehend*; to pierce by flashes of insight to some inch or so of the secret, to some star to which he can hitch his waggon. Now there are," Poetry goes on, "certain men, granted to dwell among us, of more delicate mental fibre than their fellows; men whose minds have as it were exquisite filaments which they throw out to intercept, *apprehend* and conduct home to Man stray messages between the outer mystery of the Universe and the inner mystery of his soul; even as modern telegraphy has learnt to search out, snatch and gather home messages wandering astray over waste waters of Ocean. Such men are the poets, my servants."

"Moreover," Poetry will continue, "these men do not collect their messages as your philosophers do, by vigorous striving and learning; nor, as the priests of Baal did, by cutting themselves and crying; but by schooling their souls to harmony and awaiting the moment of apprehension with what one of them has called 'a wise passiveness.' For it is not their method to wrestle with God, like Jacob, or to hold Him up with a 'Stand and deliver.' It is enough for them to be receptacles of His passing breath, as the harps abandoned and hung on willow-trees by the waters of Babylon may have caught, at evening, and hummed the wind whispering from Israel. And for this, while they hang and wait, they will be despised by the commonalty for indolent fellows, as indeed they are; as when the wind inspires and sets them hymning, they will be accused of insobriety. Yet always they excel your philosophers, insomuch as they accept the transcendental as really transcendental and do not profess to instruct the Almighty in it; and chiefly, perhaps, they excel your philosophers by opposing a creativeness, potential at any rate, against a certain and foredoomed barrenness. For the philosophers would get at the secret by reason, contemning emotion; whereas the poet knows that creation implies fatherhood, and fatherhood implies emotion, even passionate emotion. It is (take it as a cold fact) only on the impulse of yearning, on the cry of Abba, that the creature can leap to any real understanding of the Creator."

Yet the philosopher will go on to the end of time despising the poet, who grasps at mysteries *per saltum*, neglecting the military road of logic.

Shall we then, by a violent recoil, abandon Mathematics and Philosophy and commit our faith to Music? Music is, above all things, harmonious: Music has the emotion in which Mathematics and Philosophy have been found wanting. Music can be "personal"; Music, since the invention of counterpoint, is capable of harmonies deeper and more intricate than any within the range of human speech. In short, against Poetry, Music can set up a very strong claim.

But first we note that--securus judicat orbis terrarum--in the beginning Poetry and Music did their business together (with the Dance conjoined as third partner); and that, by practice, men have tended to trust Poetry, for an interpreter, more and more above Music, while Dancing has dropped out of the competition. The ballad, the sonnet, have grown to stand on their merits as verse, though their names--ballata, sonata--imply that they started in dependence upon dance and orchestra. This supersession of music by verse, whether as ally or competitor, is a historical fact, if a startling one, which Mr. Watts-Dunton, in his famous article on Poetry in the ***Encyclopaedia Britannica***, has been at pains to examine. He starts by admitting a little more than I should grant. "There is one great point of superiority," says he, "that musical art exhibits over metrical art. This consists, not in the capacity for melody, but in the capacity for harmony in the musician's sense...." "Why, of course," is my comment upon this: "every art can easily claim excellence, if it take that excellence in its own sense." Mr. Watts-Dunton proceeds: "The finest music of AEschylus, of Pindar, of Shakespeare, of Milton, is after all, only a succession of melodious notes, and in endeavouring to catch the harmonic intent of strophe, antistrophe and epode in the Greek chorus and in the true ode (that of Pindar), we can only succeed by pressing memory into our service." But I, for one, should not seek counterpoint in these any more than in the recurrent themes of a sonata. I should seek it rather in the running line which he pronounces (mistakenly, as I think) to be "after all, only a succession of melodious notes." C sharp, B, A, A, A, E, A are a succession of melodious notes and spell the opening phrase of "The Death of Nelson": as the vowels E, O, U, U, O, O, E, E, U are a succession of melodious notes, and, if notes alone counted, would spell a phrase of Milton's great Invocation to Light. But when we consider the consonantal value, the interplay and the exquisite repetition of--

Seasons return; but not to me returns
Day,...

or note the vowel-peals throughout the passage, now shut and anon opened by the scheme of consonants; now continuous, anon modulated by delicate pauses; always chiming obediently to the strain of thought; then I hold that if we have not actual counterpoint here, we have something remarkably like it,--as we certainly have harmony--

thoughts that move
Harmonious numbers,

or I know not what harmony is. In truth, if counterpoint be (as the dictionary defines it), "a blending of related but independent melodies," then Poetry achieves it by mating a process of sound to a process of thought: and Mr. Watts-Dunton disposes of his own first contention for music when he goes on to say (very rightly), "But if Poetry falls behind Music in rhythmic scope, it is capable of rendering emotion after emotion has become disintegrated into thoughts." Yet I should still object to the word "disintegrated" as applied to thought, unless it be allowed that emotion undergoes the same process at the same time and both meet in one solution. To speak more plainly, Music is inferior to Poetry because, of any two melodies in its counterpoint, both may be (and in practice are) emotional and vague: while of any two melodies in the counterpoint of Poetry one must convey thought and therefore be intelligible. And, to speak summarily, Poetry surpasses Music because it carries its explanation, whereas the meaning of a concerto has to be interpreted into dull words on a programme.

We have arrived at this, then; that Poetry's chief function is to reconcile the inner harmony of Man (his Soul, as we call it) with the outer harmony of the Universe. With this conception of "peerless Poesie" in our minds, we turn to Aristotle's *Poetics*, and it gives us a sensible shock to read on the first page, that "Epic Poetry and Tragedy, Comedy also and dithyrambic Poetry, and the greater part of the music of the flute and of the lyre are all, generally speaking, modes of imitation" ([Greek: ***pasai tynchhanoysin ohysai mimheseis to hynolon***]). "What?" we say--"Nothing better than ***that***?"--for "imitation" has a bad name among men and is apt to suggest the ape. But, first bearing in mind that there are imitations and imitations (the ***Imitatio Christi*** among them), let us go on to see what it is that in Aristotle's opinion Poetry imitates or copies. It is "the Universal" ([Greek: ***tho chathholoy***]): and as soon as we realise this we know ourselves to be on the same track as Aristotle, after all. "Imitation," as he uses it, is not an apish or a slavish imitation; it is no mere transcribing or copying of phenomena as they pass (he even allows that the poet may "imitate" men as "better than they are"): it is an expressing, in fiction and harmonious speech, intelligible to his fellow-men, of what truth, order, harmony, and "law" the poet's mind has apprehended in the outer Universe. No fair-minded reader of the ***Poetics***, as he lays down the treatise, will doubt that this, or something like this, was Aristotle's meaning, nor is it probable that he will find any essential difference (or any difference that seriously disturbs agreement) between Aristotle's "Universal" and the Platonic "Idea" or pattern of things "laid up somewhere in the heavens."

*   *   *   *   *

Now the Poet's way of apprehending the Universal is (as I have indicated) by keeping true to himself, attending to his soul's inner harmony, and listening, waiting, brooding with a "wise passiveness" until the moment when his and the larger harmony fall into tune together. The Psalmist describes the process accurately: "While I was thus musing the fire kindled, and at the last I spake with my tongue." "Poetry," writes Shelley, "is not, like reasoning, a power to be exerted according to the determination of the will. A man cannot say, *I will compose poetry*. The greatest poet, even, cannot say it: for the mind in creation is as a fading coal, which some invisible influence, like an inconstant wind, awakens to transitory brightness." But the Poet's way of reporting these apprehensions to his fellows, since he deals with Universals or ideas, is by "universalising" or "idealising" his story: and upon these two terms, which properly mean much the same thing, we must pause for a moment.

The word "idealise," which is the more commonly used, has unfortunately two meanings, a true and a false; and, again unfortunately, the false prevails in vulgar use. To "idealise" in the true sense is to disengage an "idea" of all that is trivial or impertinent or transient or disturbing, and present it to men in its clearest outline, so that its own proper form shines in on the intelligence, as you would wipe away from a discovered statue all stains or accretions of mud or moss or fungus, to release and reveal its true beauty. False "idealising," on the other hand, means that, instead of trusting to this naked manifestation, we add to it some graces of our invention, some touches by which we think to improve it; that we "paint the lily," in short. But the true "idealisation" and the first business of the poet is a denuding not an *investing* of the Goddess, whether her name be "Life," "Truth," "Beauty," or what you will: a revealing, not a coverture of embroidered words, however pretty and fantastic; as has been excellently said by Shelley: "A poem *is the very image of life expressed in its external truth*. There is this difference between a story and a poem, that a story is a catalogue of detached facts, which have no other connection than time, place, circumstance, cause and effect; the other is the erection of actions according to the unchangeable forms of human nature, as existing in the mind of the Creator, which is itself the image of all other minds." Let us enforce this account of the true idealisation by a verse or two of our old friend Sir John Davies (quoted by Coleridge in his *Biographia*

Literaria). "What an unworldly mass of impressions the mind would be," says Sir John in effect, "did not the soul come to the rescue and reduce these crowding bodies by 'sublimation strange.'"--

> *From their gross Matter she abstracts the Forms,*
> *And draws a kind of Quintessence from things,*
> *Which to her proper nature she transforms*
> *To bear them light on her celestial wings.*
> *This doth She when from things particular*
> *She doth abstract the Universal kinds....*

But it is time to descend from these heights (such as they are) of philosophising, and illustrate the difference between true and false "idealising" in Poetry by concrete example: and no two better examples occur to me, for drawing this contrast, than Webster's **Duchess of Malfy** and Shakespeare's **Macbeth**. Each of these plays excites horror and is calculated to excite horror; both have outlived three hundred years, there or thereabouts; both may be taken as having established an indefinitely long lease on men's admiration--but to any critical mind, how different an admiration! Webster is an expert, a **virtuoso** in horrifics; in flesh-creeping effects lies his skill; and, indulging that skill, he not only paints the lily, but repaints it and daubs it yet a third time. There is no reason on earth--she has offended against no moral law on earth or in the heavens--that could possibly condemn the Duchess to the hellish tortures she is made to endure. At the worst she has married a man beneath her in station. To punish her in Webster's extravagant fashion every other character, with the whole story of the play, has to be dehumanised. To me--as I penetrate the Fourth Act--the whole business becomes ludicrous: not sanely comic, or even quite sanely absurd: but bizarre, and ridiculously bizarre at that. It has no "idea" at all, no relation to the Universal in the shape of any moral order, "law," fate, doom, destiny. It is just a box of tricks, of raw heads and bloody bones, left with the lid open. That is false "idealising";

Webster choosing his effect and "improving" it for all he was worth--which (let it be added) was a great deal.

*   *   *   *   *

Turn from ***The Duchess of Malfy*** to ***Macbeth***, and you find an English poet as sensitive of fate, doom, destiny, "law," the moral order, as ever was Aeschylus; nay, interpreting it perhaps more effectively than ever did Aeschylus. In the First Act we see it suggested to Macbeth by witchcraft (which is the personified foe of moral order) that he can achieve an ambition by an unlawful path, the ambition itself being suggested along with the way to it and growing as the way opens. We see them both communicated to a feminine mind, narrower, more intent and practical; because narrower, because more intent and practical, for the moment more courageous. (It was Eve that the Serpent, wily enough, selected to tempt.) Both Macbeth and his lady move to the deed under a law which--for a while--has usurped the true moral order and reversed it, he not without misgivings: the spectators all the while knowing the true order, yet held silent, watching the event. Outside the castle an owl hoots as Duncan is slain. The guilty man and woman creep back, whispering; and thereupon--what happens? A knocking on the door--a knocking followed by the growls of a drowsy if not drunken porter: "Here's a knocking indeed! If a man were porter of hell-gate, he should have old turning the key. (Knocking again.) Knock, knock, knock! Who's there, i' the name of Beelzebub?" The stage direction admits Macduff, who in due course is to prove the avenger of blood: but the hand that knocks, the step on the threshold, are in truth those of the moral order returning ***pede claudo***, demanding to be readmitted. From the instant of that first knock the ambitions of the pair roll back toward their doom as the law they have offended reasserts itself, and the witches' palindrome ***In girum imus noctu, ecce!*** steadily spells itself backward, letter by letter, to the awful sentence, ***Ecce ut consumimur igni!***

*   *   *   *   *

This is to "idealise" in the right sense of the word. Fixing his mind on
the Idea of two human beings, a man and a woman who trespass from the
law of the great moral powers ordering the Universe (Man along with it)
and are overtaken in that trespass and punished, Shakespeare
disencumbers it of all that is trivial, irrelevant, non-essential. He
takes the wickedest crime of which man can be guilty; not a mere naked
murder, nor even a murder for profit, but the murder of a king by his
sworn soldier, of a guest by his host, of a sleeping guest by the hand
on which he has just bestowed a diamond. Can criminality be laid barer?
He illustrates it again in two persons lifted above the common station;
and he does this not (as I think) for the practical reason for which
Aristotle seems to commend it to tragic writers--that the disasters of
great persons are more striking than those of the small fry of
mankind--that, as the height is, so will be the fall--or not for that
reason alone; but, still in the process of "idealising," because such
persons, exalted above the obscuring petty cares of life, may reasonably
be expected to see the Universe with a clearer vision than ours, to have
more delicate ears for its harmonies. Who but a King should know most
concerning moral law? Why is he with our consent lifted up so that he
may hear the divine commandments better than we, and dictate them down
to us? He is greater, but yet--and this is the point--a man like
ourselves ([Greek: **omoios**]). He cannot for purposes of tragedy be
wholly good: for not only is this extremely rare in real life, and
almost inconceivable, but the ruin of a wholly good man would merely
shock, without teaching us anything. The disaster of a tragic figure
must come, and be seen to come, through some fault--or, at least, some
mistake--of his own. But again he must not be wholly bad, for the
disasters of the wholly bad do not affect us save with disgust. Such
men, we know, are not *like ourselves*. What happens to them may serve

for *The Police News*. Tragedy does not deal with the worthless. How then are Macbeth and Lady Macbeth, beings like ourselves, to fall into crime so heinous? Again Shakespeare strips the Idea bare: their trespass comes through ambition, "last infirmity of noble minds," under the blinding persuasion of witchcraft, which (an actual belief in Shakespeare's time) is a direct negation of the moral law, and puts Satan in place of God.

*   *   *   *   *

It is curious that, some thirty-odd years after Shakespeare had handled this tremendous theme, another attempt on it was being meditated, and by the man whom the most of us rank next after Shakespeare in the hierarchy of English poets. Among the treasures in the library at Trinity College, Cambridge, lies a manuscript, the hand-writing undoubtedly Milton's, containing a list compiled by him of promising subjects for the great poem for which, between his leaving the University and the outbreak of the Civil War, all his life was a deliberate preparation. The list is long; the subjects proposed run to no fewer than ninety-nine. Of these, fifty-three are derived from Old Testament history (with a recurring inclination for the theme of *Paradise Lost*), eight from the New Testament; thirty-three from the history of Britain (with a leaning towards the Arthurian legend); while five of them are legendary tales of Scotland or North Britain, the last being headed "Macbeth. Beginning at the arrival of Malcolm at Macduff. The matter of Duncan may be expressed by the arrival of his ghost." Now that Milton (an adorer of Shakespeare's genius, as everyone knows) should have taken so deep an impression from the play that its theme possessed him and he longed to transfer it to *Epic*, is credible enough. That he, with his classical bent, should choose to attempt in Drama an improvement upon the most "classical" of all Shakespeare's tragedies seems to me scarcely credible. But if the credibility of this be granted, then I can only conceive Milton's designing to improve the play by making it yet more "classical," *i.e.* by writing it (after the fashion he followed in Samson Agonistes) closely upon the model of Athenian Tragedy.

For my part I always consider Milton's **Macbeth** the most fascinating poem--certainly, if play it were, the most fascinating play--ever unwritten. But of this any man may be sure; that (since they were both great poets) one made, as the other would have made, a story of far more value to us than Shakespeare or Milton or any man before or after could have made by a strict biography of Macbeth, the man as he lived. For any such biography would clog the lesson for us with details which were more the less irrelevant because they really happened. Here I must quote Aristotle again, and for the last time in this little book: but no sentences in his treatise hold a deeper import than these:--

"It is not the function of the Poet to relate what has happened, but what may happen of likelihood or must happen of necessity. The Poet and the Historian are not different because one writes in verse and the other in prose. Turn what Herodotus tells into verse, and none the less it will be a sort of history; the metre makes no difference. The real difference lies in the Historian's telling what has happened, the Poet's telling what may happen. *Thus Poetry is a more philosophical thing, and a more serious, than History: for Poetry tells of the Universal, History of the Particular*. Now the business of the Universal is to tell us how it will fall to such and such a person to speak or act in such or such circumstances according to likelihood or necessity: and it is at this that Poetry aims in giving characters names of its own: whereas the Particular narrates what Alcibiades did or what happened to him."

        *   *   *   *   *

This may seem a hard saying, even after what has been said. So let us pause and digest it in Sir Philip Sidney's comment: "... Thus farre Aristotle, which reason of his (as all his) is most full of reason. For indeed, if the question were whether it were better to have a particular acte truly or falsely set down, there is no doubt which is to be chosen, no more than whether you had rather have **Vespasian's** picture right as hee was or at the Painter's pleasure nothing resembling. But if the question be for your owne use and learning, whether it be better to have it set downe as it should be, or as it was, then certainly is more doctrinable the fayned **Cyrus of Xenophon** than the true **Cyrus in Justine**, and the fayned **AEneas in Virgil** than the true **AEneas** in **Dares Phrygius.**"

        *   *   *   *   *

But now, having drawn breath, let us follow our Poet from the lowest up to the highest of his claim. And be it observed, to start with, that in clearing and cleansing the Idea for us (in the manner described) he does but employ a process of Selection which all men are employing, all day long and every day of their lives, upon more trivial matters; a process indeed which every man is constantly obliged to employ. Life would be a night-mare for him, soon over, if he had to take account, for example, of every object flashed on the retina of his eye during a country walk. How many millions of leaves, stones, blades of grass, must he not see without seeing? Say it be the shortest of rambles on an afternoon in early November. The light fades early: but before he reaches home in the dark, how many of the myriad falling leaves has he counted?--a dozen at most. Of the myriad leaves changing colour does he preserve, unless by chance, the separate image of one? Rather from the mass over which his eyes have travelled he has abstracted an "idea" of autumnal colouring--yellow, red, brown--and with that he carries home a sentimental, perhaps even a profound, sense of the falling leaf, the falling close of the year. So--and just so, save more deftly--the Poet abstracts:--

Where is the prime of Summer--the green prime--
The many, many leaves all twinkling?--Three
On the moss'd elm; three on the naked lime
Trembling; and one upon the old oak tree!

(As a matter of fact, oak leaves are singularly tenacious, and the autumnal oak will show a thousand for the elm's one. Hood, being a Cockney, took his seven leaves at random. But what does it matter? He was a poet, and seven leaves sufficed him to convey the idea.)

*   *   *   *   *

Nor does our Poet, unless he be a charlatan, pretend to bring home some hieratic message above the understanding of his fellows: for he is an interpreter, and the interpreter's success depends upon hitting his hearer's intelligence. Failing that, he misses everything and is null. To put it in another way--at the base of all Literature, of all Poetry, as of all Theology, stands one rock: ***the very highest Universe Truth is something so absolutely simple that a child can understand it.*** This is what Emerson means when he tells us that the great writers never *seem to condescend*; that yonder slip of a boy who has carried off Shakespeare to the window-seat, can feel with King Harry or Hamlet or Coriolanus, with Rosalind or Desdemona or Miranda. For the moment he is any given one of these, because any human soul contains them all. And some such thought we must believe to have been in Our Lord's mind when He said, "I thank Thee, O Father, Lord of heaven and earth, that

Thou hast hidden these things from the wise and prudent, and hast revealed them unto babes." For as the Universe is one, so the individual human souls that apprehend it have no varying values intrinsically, but one equal value. They differ only in power to apprehend, and this may be more easily hindered than helped by the conceit begotten of finite knowledge. I would even dare to quote of this Universal Truth the words I once hardily put into the mouth of John Wesley concerning divine Love: "I see now that if God's love reaches up to every star and down to every poor soul on Earth, it must be something vastly simple, so simple that all dwellers on earth may be assured of it--as all who have eyes may be assured of the planet shining yonder at the end of the street--and so vast that all bargaining is below it, and they may inherit it without considering their deserts." The message, then, which one Poet brings home, is no esoteric one: as Johnson said of Gray's *Elegy*, "it abounds with images which find a mirror in every mind, and with sentiments to which every bosom returns an echo." It exalts us through the best in us, by telling it, not as anything new or strange, ***but so as we recognise it***.

*   *   *   *   *

And here let us dwell a moment on Johnson's phrase, "to which every bosom returns an echo": for it recalls us to a point, which we noted indeed on p. 22, but have left (I fear) somewhat under-emphasised--the emotion that enters into poetical truth, which only by the help of emotion is apprehended; as through emotion it is conveyed, and to an emotional understanding in the hearer addresses its appeal. For the desire of man's soul after the Universal, to be in harmony with it, is (as a matter of fact, and when all pulpit eloquence has been discounted) something more than a mere intellectual attraction: a [Greek: *storghe*] rather; a yearning felt in its veins to know its fatherhood. Saint Paul goes farther and assures us that "the earnest expectation of the creature waiteth for the manifestation," so that "the whole creation groaneth and travaileth in pain together until now." "And not only they," he goes on, "but ourselves also": while the pagan poet has tears that reach the heart of the transitory show: ***Sunt lacrimae rerum, et mentem mortalia tangunt***--"Tears are for Life, mortal things pierce the soul."

And why not? For the complete man--totus homo--has feelings as well as reason, and should have both active, in fine training, to realise the best of him. Shelley obviously meant this when he defined Poetry as "the record of the best and happiest moments of the happiest and best minds." He did not mean that they are happy only in the sense of being "fortunate," ***felices***, in such moments, but that they were happy in the sense of being "blessed," ***beati***; and this feeling of blessedness they communicate. "We are aware," he goes on, "of evanescent visitations of thought and feeling sometimes associated with place or person, sometimes requiring our own mind alone, and always arising unforeseen and departing unbidden, but elevating ***and delightful*** beyond all expression ... so that even in the desire and the regret they leave, ***there cannot but be pleasure***, participating as it does in the nature of its object. It is as it were the interpenetration of a divine nature through our own, ... and the state of mind produced is at war with every base desire. The ***enthusiasm*** of virtue, love, patriotism, and friendship is essentially linked with such emotions; and whilst they last, self appears as what it is--an atom in the universe." Every word italicised above by me carries Shelley's witness that Poetry and joyous emotion are inseparable. "Poetry," he winds up, "redeems from decay the visitations of the Divinity in Man." How can we dissociate from joy the news of such visitations either on the lips that carry or in the ears that receive?

Yet, as has been hinted, the very simplicity of it puzzles the ordinary man, and not only puzzles the philosopher but exasperates him. It annoys the philosopher, first, that the poet apparently takes so little

trouble. (As a fact he takes endless trouble; but, to be sure, he saves
an immense deal by going the right way to work.) All knowledge is
notoriously painful (that is to say, to philosophers). Moreover, the
fellow mixes it up with emotion (an integral part of man which
philosophy ignores, and stultifies itself, as a rule, by ignoring). He
is one with the Oracles, a suspected tribe. He idles like an Oracle,
attending on inspiration, and when he has received the alleged afflatus,
the fellow--so different from us--is neither to hold nor to bind. The
easiest way with him seems to be a pitying contempt. "For all good
poets," says Socrates sagely in the Ion, "epic as well as lyric, compose
their lovely strains, not by art, but because they are inspired and
possessed. And as the Corybantian dances are not quite 'rational,' so
the lyric poets are, so to speak, not quite 'all there.' ... They tell
us," he goes on condescendingly, "that they bring songs from honeyed
fountains, culling them from the gardens and dells of the Muses; that,
like the bees, they wing from one flower to another. Yes of a truth: the
Poet is a light and a winged and a holy thing, without invention in him
until he is inspired and out of his senses, and out of his own wit;
until he has attained to this he is but a feeble thing, unable to utter
his oracles." I can imagine all this reported to Homer in the Shades and
Homer answering with a smile: "Well, and who in the world is denying it?
I certainly did not, while I lived and sang upon earth. Nay, I never
even sang, but invited the Muse to sing to me and through me. [Greek:
Menin haeide theha ... Handra moi hennepe, Moysa.]--Surely the dear
fellow might remember the first line of my immortal works! And if he
does remember, and is only bringing it up against me that in the
intervals of doing my work in life I was a feeble fellow, go back and
tell him that it is likely enough, yet I fail to see how it can be any
business of his, since it was only my work that I ever asked for
recognition. They say that I used to go about begging a dinner on the
strength of it. Did I?... I cannot remember. Anyhow, that nuisance is
over sometime ago, and *his* kitchen is safe!"

To you, who have followed the argument of this little book, the theory of poetic "inspiration" will be intelligible enough. It earned a living in its day and, if revived in ours, might happily supersede much modern chatter about art and technique. For it contains much truth:--

> *When the flicker of London sun falls faint on the Club-room's green*
> *   and gold,*
> * The sons of Adam sit them down and scratch with their pens in the*
> *mould--*
> *They scratch with their pens in the mould of their graves, and the ink*
> *   and the anguish start,*
> *For the Devil mutters behind the leaves, "It's pretty, but is it Art?"*

The philosophers did poetry no great harm by being angry with it as an "inspired" thing: for that, in a measure, it happens to be. They did it far more harm when they took it seriously and made it out to be a form of ***teaching***. For by the nature of things there happens to be something of the pedant in every philosopher and the incurable propensity of the pedant is to remove everything--but Literature especially--out of the category to which it belongs and consider it in another with which it has but a remote concern. (Thus a man will talk of Chaucer as though his inflexions were the most important thing about him.) Now to acclaim Homer as a great teacher, and use him in the schools, was right enough so long as the Athenians remembered (and is right enough for us, so long as we remember) ***how*** he teaches us, or rather ***educates***. What we have described the Poet as doing for men--drawing forth the inner harmonies of the soul and attuning them to the Universal--is ***educative*** in the truest sense as in the highest degree. So long as we remember this, the old dispute whether the aim of Poetry be to teach or to delight is seen to be futile: for she does both, and she does the one by means of the other. On the other hand, you cannot leave a delicate instrument such as Poetry lying within reach of the professional teacher; he will

certainly, at any risk of marring or mutilating, seize on it and use it
as a hammer to knock things into heads; if rebuked for this, plaintively
remonstrating, "But I thought you told me it was useful to teach with!"
(So Gideon taught the men of Succoth.) And therefore, we need not be
astonished: coming dawn to Strabo, to find him asserting that "the
ancients held poetry to be a kind of elementary philosophy, introducing
us from childhood to life and pleasureably instructing us in character,
behaviour and action." The Greeks, he tells us, chose poetry for their
children's first lessons. Surely (he argues) they never did that for the
sake of sweetly influencing the soul, but rather for the correction of
morals! Strabo's mental attitude is absurd, of course, and preposterous:
for this same influencing of the soul--[Greek: ***phychagoghia***] (a
beautiful word)--is, as we have seen, Poetry's main business: but the
mischief of the notion did not end with making the schooldays of
children unhappy: it took hold of the poets themselves, and by turning
them into prigs dried up the children's well of consolation. The Fathers
of the Church lent a hand too, and a vigorous one; and for centuries the
face of the Muse was sicklied o'er with a pale determination to combine
amusement with instruction. Even our noble Sidney allowed his modesty to
be overawed by the pedantic tradition, though as a man of the world he
tactfully gave it the slip. "For suppose it be granted," he says, "(that
which I suppose with great reason may be denied) that the Philosopher in
respect of his methodical proceeding doth teach more perfectly than the
Poet: yet do I thinke that no man is so much ***Philosophus*** as to compare
the Philosopher, in ***mooving***, with the Poet. And that mooving is of a
higher degree than teaching, it may by this appeare: that it is welnigh
the cause and the effect of teaching. For who will be taught, if hee bee
not mooved with desire to be taught?" Then, after a page devoted to
showing "which constant desire whosoever hath in him hath already past
halfe the hardness of the way," Sidney goes on: "Now therein of all
Sciences (I speak still of human, and according to the human conceit) is
our Poet the Monarch. For he dooth not only show the way, but giveth so
sweete a prospect into the way, as will intice any man to enter into it.

Nay he dooth as if your journey should lye through a fayre Vineyard, at the first give you a cluster of Grapes, that full of that taste you may long to passe further. He beginneth not with obscure definitions, which must blur the margent with interpretations and load the memory with doubtfulnesse: but hee commeth to you with words set in delightful proportion, either accompanied with, or prepared for, the well-inchaunting skill of Musicke; and with a tale forsooth he commeth unto you: with a tale which holdeth children from play and old men from the chimney-corner."

* * * * *

"And with a tale, forsooth, he commeth to you."--For having stripped the Idea bare, he has to reclothe it again and in such shape as will strike forcibly on his hearer's senses. A while back we broke off midway in a stanza of Sir John Davies. Let us here complete it. There are two versions. As first Davies wrote:--

This doth She when from things particular,
She doth abstract the Universal kinds,
    Which bodiless and immaterial are,
And can be lodged but only in our minds.

--the last two lines of which are weak and unnecessary. Revising the stanza, he wrote:--

This does She, when from individual states
She doth abstract the Universal kinds,
    Which then reclothed in divers names and fates
Steal access through our senses to our minds,

--which exactly describes the whole process. Having laid bare the Idea, our Poet, turning from analysis to synthesis, proceeds to reclothe it in new particulars of his own inventing, carefully chosen that they may strike home hardest upon the hearer's perceptions. Now that which strikes home hardest on a man is a tale which he can grasp by the concretest images conveyed in the concretest language. 'Labor improbus omnia vincit' tells him not half so much as a tale of the labours of Hercules; so he will learn more of patience from Job or Griselda; more of chivalrous courage from Hector or Roland or Launcelot or the tale of Palamon and Arcite; more of patriotism from the figures in history--Leonidas, Horatius, Regulus, Joan of Arc, William Tell, Garibaldi, Gordon--that have translated the Idea back into their own lives with the noblest simplicity, so that we say of them that they are "epical figures" or "figures worthy of romance," thereby paying them the highest compliment in our power: yes and more of Christian simplicity from my Uncle Toby, Colonel Newcome, even Mr. Pickwick; than from a hundred copybook maxims concerning these virtues: all these figures indeed illustrating the tritest copybook maxim of all--that "Example is better than Precept." Thus Charles Lamb praises the Plays of Shakespeare as "enrichers of the fancy, strengtheners of virtue, a withdrawing from all selfish and mercenary thoughts, a lesson of all sweet and honourable thoughts and actions, to teach courtesy, benignity, generosity, humanity: for," say he, "of **examples**, teaching those virtues, his pages are full."

*   *   *   *   *

The Poet then, having seized on the Idea and purged it of what is trivial or accidental, reclothes it in a concrete dress and so represents it to us. And you will generally remark in the very greatest poets that not only are the images they represent to us extraordinarily definite and concrete and therefore vivid--as Dante, for example, will describe a Scene in Hell or in Paradise with as much particularity as though he were writing a newspaper report; but this concreteness of vision translates itself into a remarkable concreteness of speech. I suppose there was never a more concrete writer than Shakespeare, and his practice of translating all his idea into things which you can touch or see grew steadily stronger throughout his career, so that any competent critic can in a moment distinguish his later writing from his earlier by its compression of images in words, its forcible concretion of the various "parts of speech," its masterful *corvee* of nouns substantive to do the work of verbs, and so on. Even in very early work such as Venus and Adonis we cannot but note this gift of vision, how quick and particular it is....

> *Upon this promise did he raise his chin,*
> *Like a dive-dipper, peering through a wave,*
> *Who, being look'd on, ducks as quickly in....*

But in his later plays--so fast the images teem--he has to reach out among nouns, verbs, adverbs, with both strong hands, grasping what comes and packing it ere it can protest. Take for example:--

Sleep that knits up the ravell'd sleeve of care.

Or--

> *The multitudinous sea incarnadine,*
> *Making the green one red.*

Or--

In the dark backward and abysm of time.

Or this from Lear:--

> *My face I'll grime with filth,*
> *Blanket my loins, elf all my hair in knots*
> *And with presented nakedness outface*
> *The winds and persecutions of the sky.*

Or (for vividness) this, from **Antony and Cleopatra**, when Cleopatra cries out and faints over Antony's body:--

> *O! withered is the garland of the war,*
> *The soldier's pole is fall'n: young boys and girls*
> *Are level now with men; the odds is gone,*
> *And there is nothing left remarkable*
> *Beneath the visiting moon ...*

"Madam! Madam!" "Royal Egypt!" "Empress!" cry the waiting-maids as she swoons. She revives and rebukes them:--

> *No more, but e'en a woman, and commanded*
> *By such poor passion as the maid that milks*
> *And does the meanest chares. It were for me*
> *To throw my sceptre at the injurious gods;*
> *To tell them that this world did equal theirs*
> *Till they had stolen my jewel.*

When a poet can, as Shakespeare does here, seize upon a Universal truth and lay it bare; when, apprehending **passion** in this instance, he can show it naked, the master of gods and levelling queens with milkmaids--totus est in armis idem quando nudus est Amor; when he can reclothe it in the sensuous body of Cleopatra, "Royal Egypt," and, rending the robe over that bosom, reveal the Idea again in a wound so vividly that almost we see the nature of woman spirting, like brood, against the heaven it defies; then we who have followed the Poet's ascending claims arrive at his last and highest, yet at one which has lain implicit all along in his title. He is a Poet--a "Maker." By that name, "Maker," he used to be known in English, and he deserves no lesser one.

*   *   *   *   *

I have refrained in these pages, and purposely, from technical talk and from defining the differences between Epic, Dramatic, Lyric Poetry: between the Ode and the Sonnet, the Satire and the Epigram. To use the formula of a famous Headmaster of Winchester, "details can be arranged," when once we have a clear notion of what Poetry is, and of what by nature it aims to do. My sole intent has been to clarify that notion, which (if the reader has been patient to follow me) reveals the Poet as a helper of man's most insistent spiritual need and therefore as a member most honourable in any commonwealth: since, as Ben Jonson says: "Every beggarly corporation affords the State a mayor or two bailiffs yearly; but ***solus rex, aut poeta, non quotannis nascitur***"--these two only, a King and a Poet, are not born every year. The Poet "makes"--that is to say, creates--which is a part of the divine function; and he makes--using man's highest instruments, thought and speech--harmonious inventions that answer the harmony we humbly trace in the firmament fashioned, controlled, upheld, by divine wisdom. *"Non c'e' in mondo,"* said Torquato Tasso proudly, ***"chi merita nome di creatore, se non Iddio ed il Poeta"***--"Two beings only deserve the name of Creator: God and the Poet."

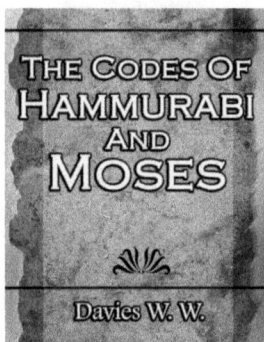

The Codes Of Hammurabi And Moses
W. W. Davies

The discovery of the Hammurabi Code is one of the greatest achievements of archaeology, and is of paramount interest, not only to the student of the Bible, but also to all those interested in ancient history...

Religion   ISBN: *1-59462-338-4*   **Pages:132**

MSRP $12.95

QTY

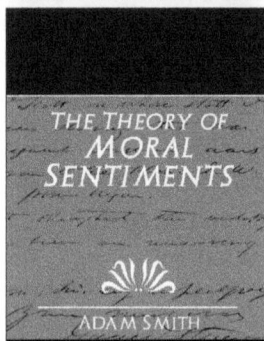

The Theory of Moral Sentiments
Adam Smith

This work from 1749. contains original theories of conscience amd moral judgment and it is the foundation for systemof morals.

Philosophy ISBN: *1-59462-777-0*   **Pages:536**

MSRP $19.95

QTY

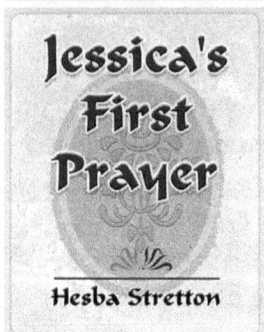

Jessica's First Prayer
Hesba Stretton

In a screened and secluded corner of one of the many railway-bridges which span the streets of London there could be seen a few years ago, from five o'clock every morning until half past eight, a tidily set-out coffee-stall, consisting of a trestle and board, upon which stood two large tin cans, with a small fire of charcoal burning under each so as to keep the coffee boiling during the early hours of the morning when the work-people were thronging into the city on their way to their daily toil...

Childrens   ISBN: *1-59462-373-2*   **Pages:84**

MSRP $9.95

QTY

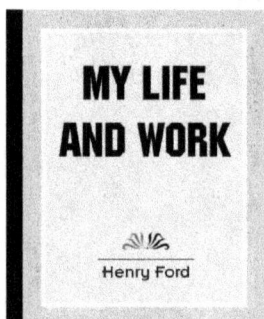

My Life and Work
Henry Ford

Henry Ford revolutionized the world with his implementation of mass production for the Model T automobile. Gain valuable business insight into his life and work with his own auto-biography... "We have only started on our development of our country we have not as yet, with all our talk of wonderful progress, done more than scratch the surface. The progress has been wonderful enough but..."

Biographies/ ISBN: *1-59462-198-5*   **Pages:300**

MSRP $21.95

QTY

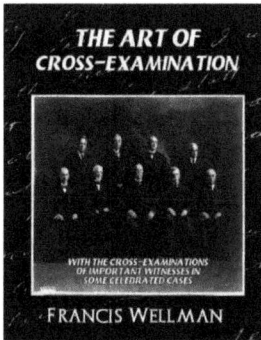

The Art of Cross-Examination
Francis Wellman

QTY

I presume it is the experience of every author, after his first book is published upon an important subject, to be almost overwhelmed with a wealth of ideas and illustrations which could readily have been included in his book, and which to his own mind, at least, seem to make a second edition inevitable. Such certainly was the case with me; and when the first edition had reached its sixth impression in five months, I rejoiced to learn that it seemed to my publishers that the book had met with a sufficiently favorable reception to justify a second and considerably enlarged edition. ..

Pages:412

Reference   ISBN: *1-59462-647-2*   *MSRP $19.95*

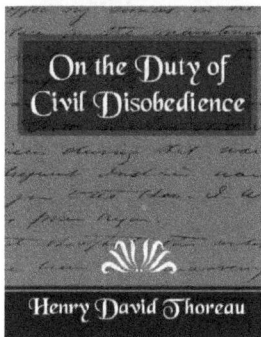

On the Duty of Civil Disobedience
Henry David Thoreau

QTY

Thoreau wrote his famous essay, On the Duty of Civil Disobedience, as a protest against an unjust but popular war and the immoral but popular institution of slave-owning. He did more than write—he declined to pay his taxes, and was hauled off to gaol in consequence. Who can say how much this refusal of his hastened the end of the war and of slavery ?

Law   ISBN: *1-59462-747-9*   **Pages:48**   *MSRP $7.45*

Dream Psychology Psychoanalysis for Beginners
Sigmund Freud

QTY

Sigmund Freud, born Sigismund Schlomo Freud (May 6, 1856 - September 23, 1939), was a Jewish-Austrian neurologist and psychiatrist who co-founded the psychoanalytic school of psychology. Freud is best known for his theories of the unconscious mind, especially involving the mechanism of repression; his redefinition of sexual desire as mobile and directed towards a wide variety of objects; and his therapeutic techniques, especially his understanding of transference in the therapeutic relationship and the presumed value of dreams as sources of insight into unconscious desires.

Pages:196

Psychology   ISBN: *1-59462-905-6*   *MSRP $15.45*

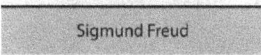

The Miracle of Right Thought
Orison Swett Marden

QTY

Believe with all of your heart that you will do what you were made to do. When the mind has once formed the habit of holding cheerful, happy, prosperous pictures, it will not be easy to form the opposite habit. It does not matter how improbable or how far away this realization may see, or how dark the prospects may be, if we visualize them as best we can, as vividly as possible, hold tenaciously to them and vigorously struggle to attain them, they will gradually become actualized, realized in the life. But a desire, a longing without endeavor, a yearning abandoned or held indifferently will vanish without realization.

Pages:360

Self Help   ISBN: *1-59462-644-8*   *MSRP $25.45*

QTY

The Rosicrucian Cosmo-Conception Mystic Christianity *by Max Heindel* ISBN: *1-59462-188-8* **$38.95**
The Rosicrucian Cosmo-conception is not dogmatic, neither does it appeal to any other authority than the reason of the student. It is: not controversial, but is: sent forth in the, hope that it may help to clear... New Age/Religion Pages 646

Abandonment To Divine Providence *by Jean-Pierre de Caussade* ISBN: *1-59462-228-0* **$25.95**
"The Rev. Jean Pierre de Caussade was one of the most remarkable spiritual writers of the Society of Jesus in France in the 18th Century. His death took place at Toulouse in 1751. His works have gone through many editions and have been republished... Inspirational/Religion Pages 400

Mental Chemistry *by Charles Haanel* ISBN: *1-59462-192-6* **$23.95**
Mental Chemistry allows the change of material conditions by combining and appropriately utilizing the power of the mind. Much like applied chemistry creates something new and unique out of careful combinations of chemicals the mastery of mental chemistry... New Age Pages 354

The Letters of Robert Browning and Elizabeth Barret Barrett 1845-1846 vol II ISBN: *1-59462-193-4* **$35.95**
by Robert Browning and Elizabeth Barrett Biographies Pages 596

Gleanings In Genesis (volume I) *by Arthur W. Pink* ISBN: *1-59462-130-6* **$27.45**
Appropriately has Genesis been termed "the seed plot of the Bible" for in it we have, in germ form, almost all of the great doctrines which are afterwards fully developed in the books of Scripture which follow... Religion/Inspirational Pages 420

The Master Key *by L. W. de Laurence* ISBN: *1-59462-001-6* **$30.95**
In no branch of human knowledge has there been a more lively increase of the spirit of research during the past few years than in the study of Psychology, Concentration and Mental Discipline. The requests for authentic lessons in Thought Control, Mental Discipline and... New Age/Business Pages 422

The Lesser Key Of Solomon Goetia *by L. W. de Laurence* ISBN: *1-59462-092-X* **$9.95**
This translation of the first book of the "Lernegton" which is now for the first time made accessible to students of Talismanic Magic was done, after careful collation and edition, from numerous Ancient Manuscripts in Hebrew, Latin, and French... New Age/Occult Pages 92

Rubaiyat Of Omar Khayyam *by Edward Fitzgerald* ISBN: *1-59462-332-5* **$13.95**
Edward Fitzgerald, whom the world has already learned, in spite of his own efforts to remain within the shadow of anonymity, to look upon as one of the rarest poets of the century, was born at Bredfield, in Suffolk, on the 31st of March, 1809. He was the third son of John Purcell... Music Pages 172

Ancient Law *by Henry Maine* ISBN: *1-59462-128-4* **$29.95**
The chief object of the following pages is to indicate some of the earliest ideas of mankind, as they are reflected in Ancient Law, and to point out the relation of those ideas to modern thought. Religiom/History Pages 452

Far-Away Stories *by William J. Locke* ISBN: *1-59462-129-2* **$19.45**
"Good wine needs no bush, but a collection of mixed vintages does. And this book is just such a collection. Some of the stories I do not want to remain buried for ever in the museum files of dead magazine-numbers an author's not unpardonable vanity..." Fiction Pages 272

Life of David Crockett *by David Crockett* ISBN: *1-59462-250-7* **$27.45**
"Colonel David Crockett was one of the most remarkable men of the times in which he lived. Born in humble life, but gifted with a strong will, an indomitable courage, and unremitting perseverance... Biographies/New Age Pages 424

Lip-Reading *by Edward Nitchie* ISBN: *1-59462-206-X* **$25.95**
Edward B. Nitchie, founder of the New York School for the Hard of Hearing, now the Nitchie School of Lip-Reading, Inc, wrote "LIP-READING Principles and Practice". The development and perfecting of this meritorious work on lip-reading was an undertaking... How-to Pages 400

A Handbook of Suggestive Therapeutics, Applied Hypnotism, Psychic Science ISBN: *1-59462-214-0* **$24.95**
by Henry Munro Health/New Age/Health/Self-help Pages 376

A Doll's House: and Two Other Plays *by Henrik Ibsen* ISBN: *1-59462-112-8* **$19.95**
Henrik Ibsen created this classic when in revolutionary 1848 Rome. Introducing some striking concepts in playwriting for the realist genre, this play has been studied the world over. Fiction/Classics/Plays 308

The Light of Asia *by sir Edwin Arnold* ISBN: *1-59462-204-3* **$13.95**
In this poetic masterpiece, Edwin Arnold describes the life and teachings of Buddha. The man who was to become known as Buddha to the world was born as Prince Gautama of India but he rejected the worldly riches and abandoned the reigns of power when... Religion/History/Biographies Pages 170

The Complete Works of Guy de Maupassant *by Guy de Maupassant* ISBN: *1-59462-157-8* **$16.95**
"For days and days, nights and nights, I had dreamed of that first kiss which was to consecrate our engagement, and I knew not on what spot I should put my lips..." Fiction/Classics Pages 240

The Art of Cross-Examination *by Francis L. Wellman* ISBN: *1-59462-309-0* **$26.95**
Written by a renowned trial lawyer, Wellman imparts his experience and uses case studies to explain how to use psychology to extract desired information through questioning. How-to/Science/Reference Pages 408

Answered or Unanswered? *by Louisa Vaughan* ISBN: *1-59462-248-5* **$10.95**
Miracles of Faith in China Religion Pages 112

The Edinburgh Lectures on Mental Science (1909) *by Thomas* ISBN: *1-59462-008-3* **$11.95**
This book contains the substance of a course of lectures recently given by the writer in the Queen Street Hall, Edinburgh. Its purpose is to indicate the Natural Principles governing the relation between Mental Action and Material Conditions... New Age/Psychology Pages 148

Ayesha *by H. Rider Haggard* ISBN: *1-59462-301-5* **$24.95**
Verily and indeed it is the unexpected that happens! Probably if there was one person upon the earth from whom the Editor of this, and of a certain previous history, did not expect to hear again... Classics Pages 380

Ayala's Angel *by Anthony Trollope* ISBN: *1-59462-352-X* **$29.95**
The two girls were both pretty, but Lucy who was twenty-one who supposed to be simple and comparatively unattractive, whereas Ayala was credited, as her Bombwhat romantic name might show, with poetic charm and a taste for romance. Ayala when her father died was nineteen... Fiction Pages 484

The American Commonwealth *by James Bryce* ISBN: *1-59462-286-8* **$34.45**
An interpretation of American democratic political theory. It examines political mechanics and society from the perspective of Scotsman James Bryce Politics Pages 572

Stories of the Pilgrims *by Margaret P. Pumphrey* ISBN: *1-59462-116-0* **$17.95**
This book explores pilgrims religious oppression in England as well as their escape to Holland and eventual crossing to America on the Mayflower, and their early days in New England... History Pages 268

QTY

The Fasting Cure *by Sinclair Upton*   ISBN: *1-59462-222-1*   **$13.95**
In the Cosmopolitan Magazine for May, 1910, and in the Contemporary Review (London) for April, 1910, I published an article dealing with my experiences in fasting. I have written a great many magazine articles, but never one which attracted so much attention... New Age/Self Help/Health Pages 164

Hebrew Astrology *by Sepharial*   ISBN: *1-59462-308-2*   **$13.45**
In these days of advanced thinking it is a matter of common observation that we have left many of the old landmarks behind and that we are now pressing forward to greater heights and to a wider horizon than that which represented the mind-content of our progenitors... Astrology Pages 144

Thought Vibration or The Law of Attraction in the Thought World   ISBN: *1-59462-127-6*   **$12.95**
by William Walker Atkinson   Psychology/Religion Pages 144

Optimism *by Helen Keller*   ISBN: *1-59462-108-X*   **$15.95**
Helen Keller was blind, deaf, and mute since 19 months old, yet famously learned how to overcome these handicaps, communicate with the world, and spread her lectures promoting optimism. An inspiring read for everyone... Biographies/Inspirational Pages 84

Sara Crewe *by Frances Burnett*   ISBN: *1-59462-360-0*   **$9.45**
In the first place, Miss Minchin lived in London. Her home was a large, dull, tall one, in a large, dull square, where all the houses were alike, and all the sparrows were alike, and where all the door-knockers made the same heavy sound... Childrens/Classic Pages 88

The Autobiography of Benjamin Franklin *by Benjamin Franklin*   ISBN: *1-59462-135-7*   **$24.95**
The Autobiography of Benjamin Franklin has probably been more extensively read than any other American historical work, and no other book of its kind has had such ups and downs of fortune. Franklin lived for many years in England, where he was agent... Biographies/History Pages 332

Name	
Email	
Telephone	
Address	
City, State ZIP	

☐ **Credit Card**   ☐ **Check / Money Order**

Credit Card Number	
Expiration Date	
Signature	

Please Mail to: Book Jungle
PO Box 2226
Champaign, IL 61825
or Fax to: 630-214-0564

ORDERING INFORMATION
web: *www.bookjungle.com*
email: *sales@bookjungle.com*
fax: *630-214-0564*
mail: *Book Jungle PO Box 2226 Champaign, IL 61825*
or PayPal *to sales@bookjungle.com*

Please contact us for bulk discounts

DIRECT-ORDER TERMS

20% Discount if You Order Two or More Books
Free Domestic Shipping!
Accepted: Master Card, Visa, Discover, American Express

www.ingramcontent.com/pod-product-compliance
Lightning Source LLC
Chambersburg PA
CBHW081947070426

42453CB00013BA/2375